The Butterfly Catcher

Courtney Cox Smith

swallowtail books
houston

Copyright © 2016 by Courtney Cox Smith

All rights reserved. No part of this publication may be reproduced in any form without written permission of the publisher.

ISBN 978-0-692-66791-0

Library of Congress Control Number: 2016904399

First Printing 2016

swallowtail books
www.swallowtailbooks.com

For Jack,
who flies with the butterflies

There once was a boy who lost his brother.
"Where is Jack?" he wondered to his mother.

One day Jack was here and the next he was gone,
and the little boy was uncertain how to go on.

"He flies with the butterflies,," his mother softly said.
"Now close your eyes and rest your head."

The next day the boy
had a wonderful thought.
"I will go and find him,"
he began to plot.

So the little boy gathered
his gear and supplies
and set out on a journey
to find butterflies.

The boy searched low,
and the boy searched high.
He searched for any butterfly
he might possibly spy.

At last he found one all alone,
resting on the smoothest pebble stone.
In a flash and with a swoosh of his net
the little boy caught the butterfly
without breaking a sweat.

The butterfly was a
beautiful black and yellow,
but he proved to be
a rather stern fellow.

He flitted and fluttered
around in the net.
Frightened and alarmed,
he was shocked and upset.

"Let me out! Let me out!"
he angrily cried.
"I demand you set me free!"
he shouted with pride.

But the boy was unmoved by the hullabaloo
as he asked the butterfly simply, "who are you?"

"Swallowtail is my name,
but this is not a game!"

"Calm down, calm down," said the little boy.
"I assure you this is not a ploy.
My brother Jack is who I seek,
I hoped he might be near this creek."

"Pfft! I do not know your Jack.
I must demand you put me back!"

But the boy ignored the
Swallowtail's haughty cries,
"Are you sure you do not know him
for he flies with butterflies?"

The Swallowtail sighed, "I simply do not know.
Now really you must let me go!"

So the boy set him free without delay,
and the Swallowtail took off and flew away.
Then the little boy gathered his things
and continued his search for butterfly wings.

He set out his cage and opened the door,
waiting patiently in hopes of catching one more.

Surprisingly, it was not long after
a butterfly appeared overcome with laughter.

"Ha, ha, ha, ha, helloooo!" she said with a chuckle,
as the boy closed the cage and fastened the buckle.

"Hello there. Who are you?"
the little boy asked without further ado.

"I am Painted Lady my dear.
Who are you and why are you here?"

"I am on a journey to find my brother Jack.
I hope to catch him and bring him back.
He flies with butterflies.
I bet he is right about your size."

"Hee, hee, hee," Painted Lady giggled with glee,
"I know not him, and he knows not me.
Little boy won't you stay and play?
We could frolic and laugh together all day."

The boy replied, "Thank you Painted Lady but no.
My search continues, so I really must go."

The little boy opened the cage door,
and away the Painted Lady flew with a cackling roar.

Onward the little boy went
with a hopeful heart and earnest intent.

Soon the boy came
upon a nearby wood.
He questioned whether
going ahead would be good.

He slowly approached
the canopy of trees,
where he heard the
tiniest of sounds with ease.

Before long the boy grew tired,
feeling lost, hungry, and uninspired.
Leaning against a nearby tree,
he looked around for what he could see.

Much to his delight,
the boy saw a most interesting sight...
a giant butterfly of yellow and green.
It was unlike anything he had ever seen.

"Excuse me, what kind of butterfly are you?"
the boy asked curiously.
Startled, the creature came alive
and answered most furiously.

"I am a moth you little fool!
Don't they teach you anything in school?
Who are you and why do you disturb my peace?
Please go away and make this talking cease!"

The little boy could see
the Moth was old and grumpy,
and his conversation was
rather sharp and bumpy.

But the little boy persisted
for he had to know if his brother existed.

"I am looking for my brother
who flies with butterflies.
You must know him for
you seem old and wise."

"The meadow ahead is where you should go,
for if you don't, you will never know.
You must add the meadow to your list.
If your brother is not there, he must not exist.
Now go away and leave me be.
Go rest your head on some other tree."

So the little boy walked until he
came upon the meadow.
Across the field were flowers
of purple, red, and yellow.

Then he looked up toward
the bright blue sky
to see it swarming with
every kind of butterfly.

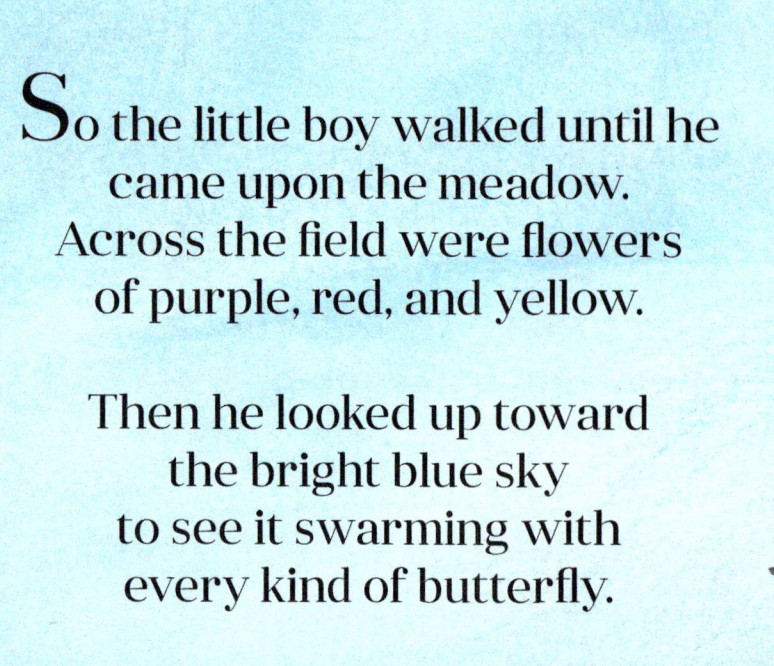

Overflowing with excitement and cheer,
the boy ran through the meadow
hoping his brother was here.

When he reached the center part,
the little boy shouted with all his heart,
"Jack, Jack? Are you here?
It's just your brother, please don't fear.
Does anyone know my brother Jack?"

The boy heard nothing but silence back.

The little boy hung his head in sadness,
it all seemed to be such madness.

Just then, a Monarch, known to be gentle and wise,
softly answered the boy's desperate cries.

"Little boy," called the Monarch,
"Little boy, you have it all wrong,
for he has been with you all along.

Jack rests on every butterfly's wings.
He is the sweet melody that each bird sings.
He is in the whispering leaves of every tree
and rides the mighty waves of the deep blue sea.
He is the shimmer of each raindrop
that falls from the sky.
He is in each baby's newborn cry.
He is in the fragrant flowers that grow
and in each flake of falling snow.
He is in the stars that twinkle at night
and in the moon's soft glowing light.

And little boy, he is in you.
Oh how I wish you knew!
He is in each giggle and laugh.
He is with you when you struggle with math.
He is there when you are sad,
and he is there when you are mad.
He goes with you as you dream
and when you enjoy your favorite ice cream.

And though you feel far apart,
he lives on always in your heart."

And then the Monarch flew away
and left the little boy to run and play.

The little boy let out a great big sigh
as he looked up to the bright blue sky.

With one little hand he held his chest,
feeling warm, happy, and simply blessed.

Now the boy's search was complete
and the ending ever so sweet,
for the little boy knew from the start
he carried his brother in his heart.

CPSIA information can be obtained
at www.ICGtesting.com
Printed in the USA
LVOW06*1015200716
497070LV00016B/89/P